DK | Penguin Random House

Written by Dawn Sirett
Illustrated by Rachael Hare, Louise Dick, Karen Hood,
Kitty Glavin, Victoria Palastanga, Kate Bull, Anna Kluska
Educational Consultant Penny Coltman
US Senior Editor Shannon Beatty
Designed by Rachael Hare, Louise Dick, Karen Hood,
Charlotte Bull, Polly Appleton, Victoria Palastanga, Claire Patane
Additional Editorial Work Sally Beets
Additional Design Work Jaileen Kaur,
Rajesh Singh Adhikari, Rajdeep Singh
Managing Editor Penny Smith
Managing Art Editor Mabel Chan
Producer, Pre-production Nadine King
Producer Inderjit Bhullar

Spanish edition
Editorial services Imanol Echeverria
Translation Sara Pineda

First American Edition, 2018
Published in the United States by DK Publishing,
1745 Broadway, 20th Floor. New York, NY 10019
A Penguin Random House Company

Original title: *1000 Useful Words*
Bilingual edition, fifth reprint: 2024
Copyright © 2018 Dorling Kindersley Limited
© Spanish translation 2019 Dorling Kindersley Limited

ISBN: 978-1-4654-8099-6

DK books are available at special discounts when purchased in bulk
for sales promotions, premiums, fund-raising, or educational use.
For details, contact: DK Publishing Special Markets,
1745 Broadway, 20th Floor. New York, NY 10019

Printed and bound in China

www.dkespañol.com

Bilingual WORDS
ENGLISH - SPANISH
1000
INGLÉS - ESPAÑOL
PALABRAS bilingües

¡pío! tweet!

DK

Introducción • Introduction

Este libro está dirigido a niños que aún no saben o están aprendiendo a leer. Las páginas contienen numerosas ilustraciones que hacen la lectura entretenida y ayudan a los niños a desarrollar sus habilidades de lectura y escritura en inglés y español.

This book can be used with children who have not yet learned to read and with beginner readers. Each picture-packed page is fun to read together, and a great way to help children's language and literacy skills in English and Spanish.

Páginas con ilustraciones y vocabulario

La mayoría de páginas contienen ilustraciones y palabras, principalmente sustantivos, pero también algunos verbos y adjetivos para que los más pequeños enriquezcan su vocabulario y conocimientos.

Picture-and-word pages

Most of this book is made up of picture-and-word pages filled with nouns, plus some verbs and adjectives. These pages help broaden your child's vocabulary and knowledge.

Páginas de cuentos

También hay cinco cuentos sencillos que presentan vocabulario cotidiano, sitúan los términos en el contexto y ayudan a desarrollar las habilidades para escribir frases y cuentos.

Story pages

There are also five simple stories to read that introduce more useful words, put words into context, and help sentence writing and story writing skills.

Cómo ayudar al niño a aprovechar al máximo este libro

Todas las páginas del libro ofrecen oportunidades para hablar y aprender: pueden disfrutar juntos explorando y conversando. Señala cosas que le gusten al niño, diciendo cosas como "¡Mira, un tigre! ¿Sabes rugir como un tigre?" o "¿Qué fruta te gusta a ti?"

Sigue el ritmo del niño, deja que lleve la iniciativa y dé vuelta las hojas. Cuando se canse, paren y retomen el libro en otra ocasión.

How to help your child get the most out of this book

All the pages in this book offer lots of opportunities for talking and learning. Enjoy exploring and talking about them together. Point out things your child likes. For instance, you could say, "Look, there's a tiger! Can you roar like a tiger?" or "Which fruit do you like?"

Go at your child's pace. Let her take the lead and turn the pages. Stop if she is tired, and return to the book another time.

Para niños que aún no saben leer

Señala las imágenes mientras lees las palabras y las frases para ayudarle a identificar las cosas y para mostrar la relación entre los dibujos y las palabras.

For children who are not yet reading

Point to the pictures as you read the words and sentences to help them identify things, and to show how the pictures and words are connected.

Para lectores principiantes

Mientras el niño lee o leen juntos, señala las palabras o anímale a señalarlas, para ayudarle a reconocer las letras y las palabras.

Seguir los cuentos

Tanto los lectores principiantes como los niños que aún no saben leer pueden seguir los cuentos pasando el dedo por las líneas de puntos. Esto les ayudará además a desarrollar la motricidad fina.

Juegos de buscar y preguntas sencillas

Hay preguntas sencillas y juegos de buscar y encontrar que fomentan el aprendizaje. Es posible que el niño requiera de tu ayuda, o que prefiera que tú también participes y respondan juntos.

Lo más importante es respetar los intereses del niño, hablar sobre cosas que sabes que le gustan, aplaudir sus respuestas y divertirse.

• • •

For children who are beginning to read

As they read, or as you read together, point to the words, or encourage them to point, to help their letter and word recognition.

Following the stories

Pre-readers and beginner readers can follow the stories by running a finger along the dotted lines. This helps their fine motor skills, too.

"Can you find?" games and simple questions

There are "Can you find?" games and simple questions on the picture-and-word pages that encourage learning. Your child may need help with these, or he may like you to join in and answer with him.

Most importantly, follow your child's interests, talk about things you know he enjoys, give lots of praise as he answers the questions, and have fun!.

Contenidos
Contents

Mi cuerpo y yo
Me and my body

¿De qué color son tus ojos?
What color are your eyes?

cara
face

ojo
eye

oreja
ear

boca
mouth

nariz
nose

dientes
teeth

pecho
chest

dedos de la mano
fingers

dedo pulgar
thumb

manos
hands

pie
foot

¿Tienes el pelo largo o corto?
Is your hair long or short?

cabeza
head

pelo
hair

cuello
neck

espalda
back

brazo
arm

trasero
bottom

pierna
leg

dedos del pie
toes

Me cuido
Taking care of myself

cepillo
hairbrush

jabón
soap

champú
shampoo

bloqueador solar
sunblock

cepillo de dientes
toothbrush

pañuelos desechable
(para sonarme la nari
tissues (for blowing my no

8

Cosas que hago
Things I do

Puedo...
I can...

sentarme
sit

pararme
stand

caminar
walk

¡bla!
chatter!

¡bla!
chatter!

hablar
talk

escuchar
listen

¡Ja, ja, ja!
hee! hee!

reír
laugh

saltar
jump

bailar
dance

hacer volteretas
roll

estirarme
stretch

equilibrarme
balance

inclinarme
bend

zapatear
stamp

aplaudir
clap

saludar con la mano
wave

Mis sentidos
My senses

tacto/tocar
touching

vista/ver
seeing

oído/oír
hearing

gusto/saborear
tasting

olfato/oler
smelling

Mi familia y amigos
My family and friends

Existen todo tipo de familias...
There are all kinds of families...

Quiero a mi familia.
I love my family.

Abuelos
Grandparents

abuelita
granny

abuela
grandmother

abue
grandma

Padres
Parents

mami
mommy

madre
mother

mamita
ma

mamá
mom

papi
daddy

padre
father

papito
pop

papá
dad

Primos
Cousins

hermana
sister

hermano
brother

niña/niño
child

bebé
baby

Cuido a mi hermanito.
I take care of my little brother.

Hermanos
Siblings

¿Quién es el más viejo en tu familia?
Who is the oldest person in your family?

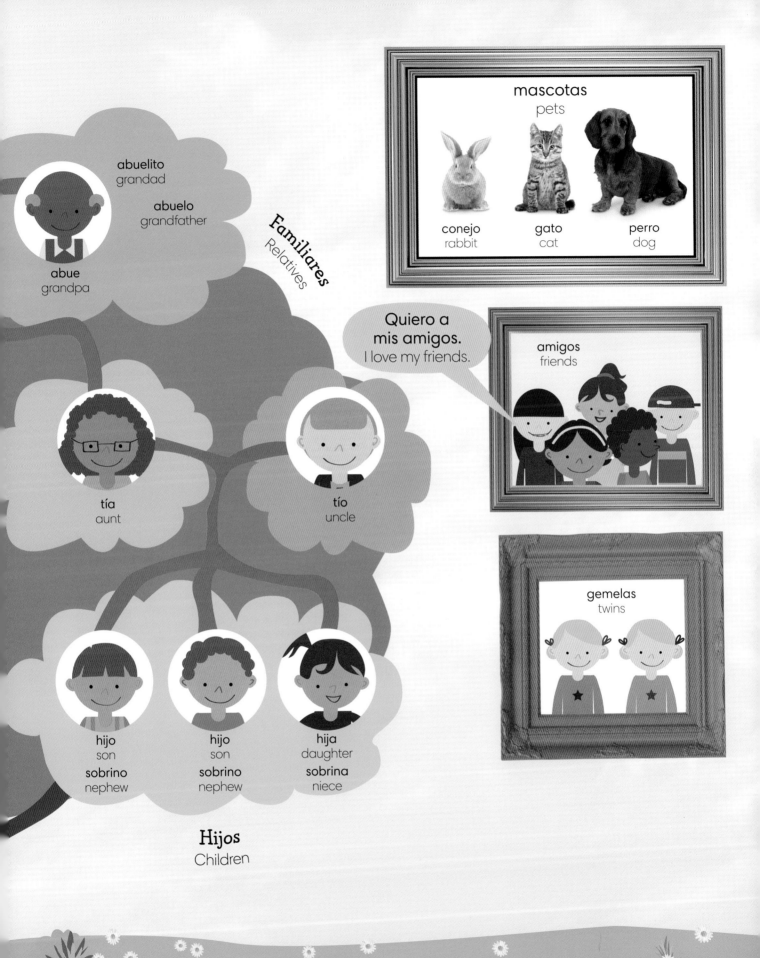

abuelito
grandad

abuelo
grandfather

abue
grandpa

Familiares
Relatives

mascotas
pets

conejo
rabbit

gato
cat

perro
dog

Quiero a
mis amigos.
I love my friends.

amigos
friends

tía
aunt

tío
uncle

gemelas
twins

hijo
son

hijo
son

hija
daughter

sobrino
nephew

sobrino
nephew

sobrina
niece

Hijos
Children

¿Quién es el más joven?
Who is the youngest?

Cosas para vestir
Things to wear

playera
T-shirt

playera sin mangas
tank top

calcetines
socks

medias
tights

calzones
underpants

vaqueros
jeans

falda
skirt

short
shorts

suéter
sweater

sombrero para el sol
sun hat

reloj
watch

pantuflas
slippers

botas
boots

guantes
gloves

sombrero de lana
woolen hat

bufanda
scarf

tenis
sneakers

zapatos
shoes

sombrero de lana
woolen hat

bufanda
scarf

copo de nieve
snowflake

Mira todas las cosas que cuelgan en el tendedero. Elige algo para ponerte en un día frío y...
Look at all the things hanging on the clotheslines. Choose something to wear on a cold day and...

12

botón
button

chaqueta
jacket

paraguas
umbrella

polar
fleece

vestido
dress

pantalones
pants

camiseta
del pijama
pajama top

short de traje de baño
swimming shorts

traje de baño
swimsuit

gafas
goggles

bolso
bag

pantalón del
pijama
pajama bottoms

collar
necklace

mochila
backpack

cierre
zipper

cinturón
belt

hebilla
buckle

monedero
purse

gorra de béisbol
baseball cap

casco para
bicicleta
bicycle helmet

disfraces
dress-up clothes

sandalias
sandals

moño para el pelo
hair bow

pasador
barrette

algo para ponerte
en un día caluroso.
something to wear
on a hot day.

lentes para el sol
sunglasses

sol
sun

13

Comida y bebidas
Food and drink

¿Qué verduras has comido hoy?
What vegetables have you eaten today?

Elige tres de estos alimentos para hacer una ensalada.
Choose three of these foods to make a salad.

Fruta
Fruit

uvas
grapes

piña
pineapple

plátano
banana

manzana
apple

limón
lemon

sandía
watermelon

papas
potatoes

fresas
strawberries

naranja
orange

ejotes
green beans

coliflor
cauliflower

zanahoria
carrot

Verduras
Vegetables

pimiento
red pepper

cebollas
onions

calabaza
pumpkin

galletas
cookies

chícharos
peas

col
cabbage

mantecadas
cupcakes

brócoli
broccoli

pasteles
pastries

helado
ice cream

Golosinas
Treats

tomate
tomato

pepino
cucumber

aceitunas
olives

lechuga
lettuce

apio
celery

14

queso
cheese

En el refrigerador
In the fridge

pollo
chicken

huevos
eggs

mantequilla
butter

pescado
fish

chorizos
sausages

yogurt
yogurt

miel
honey

pan
bread

arroz
rice

cereal
cereal

fideos
noodles

pastas
pasta

aceite
oil

harina
flour

azúcar
sugar

frutos secos
nuts

En la despensa
In the pantry

té
tea

café
coffee

leche
milk

especias
spices

agua
water

jugo
juice

Bebidas
Drinks

Elige uno de estos alimentos para hacer la comida.
Choose one of these foods to make for lunch.

hamburguesa
hamburger

sándwich
sandwich

omelette
omelet

pizza
pizza

Busca algo saludable para tu lonchera.
Find something healthy for your snack box.

15

Todo en un día
All in a day

despertador
alarm clock

mañana
morning

mesita
bedside table

cama
bed

Jack se despierta a las 8 en punto.
Jack wakes up at 8 o'clock.

Para desayunar, come avena y un plátano.
Jack eats some oatmeal and a banana for breakfast.

hora del desayuno
breakfast time

gorra
hat

chaqueta
jacket

zanahoria de juguete
toy carrot

avena
oatmeal

playera
T-shirt

plátano
banana

short
shorts

¡Su conejo de peluche también tiene comida!
His toy rabbit has food, too!

bufanda
scarf

calcetines
socks

tenis
sneakers

Luego Jack se viste.
Then Jack gets dressed.

¿Qué podrían hacer Jack y su conejo
durante el día? Elige...
What might Jack and his rabbit do during the day?
You choose...

trenes
trains

bandera
flag

guarida
den

¿Juegan con los trenes
en la mañana...
Do they play with the trains
in the morning...

o van al parque
a patinar?
or do they
scoot in
the park?

monopatín
scooter

¿Construyen una guarida por la tarde...
Do they build a den in the afternoon...

pastel
cake

u hornean un pastel?
or do they bake a cake?

noche
nighttime

hora del baño
bath time

Baño
bath

Al final del día,
es hora de bañarse y
después acostarse.
At the end of the day,
it's time for a bath.
Then it's bedtime.

pijamas
pajamas

abrazo de
buenas noches
bedtime
snuggle

A Jack y a su conejo les gusta
abrazarse para dormir.
Jack and his rabbit like to snuggle
at bedtime.

pantuflas
slippers

17

En la casa
Around the house

Encuentra cinco osos de peluche.
Find five teddy bears.

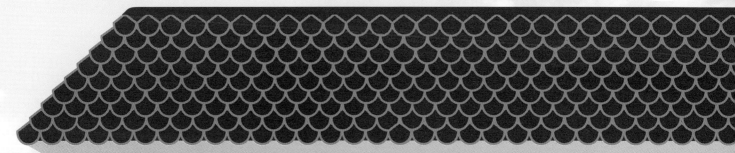

dormitorio
bedroom

almohada
pillow

cama
bed

despertador
alarm clock

lámpara
lamp

cortina
curtain

ropero
wardrobe

libros
books

ventana
window

mesita
bedside table

tapete
mat

puf
beanbag

juguetes
toys

piso
floor

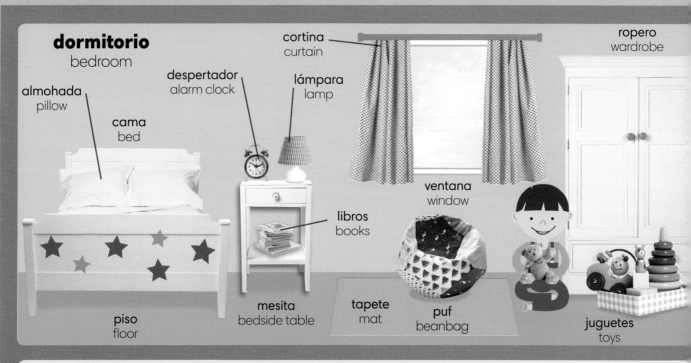

cocina
kitchen

reloj
clock

teléfono
phone

armarios
cabinets

mesa
table

cocina
stove

lavadora
washing machine

refrigerador
fridge

silla
chair

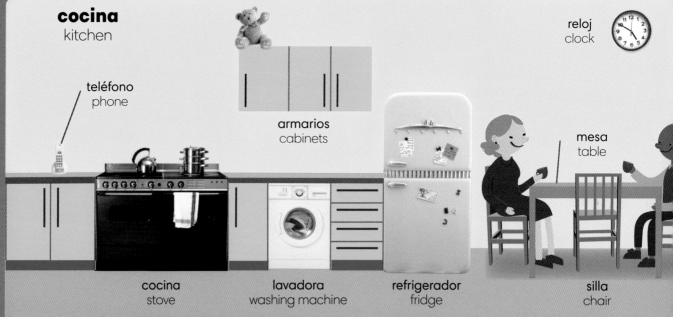

Elige un lugar cómodo para leer un libro.
Choose a cozy place to read a book.

chimenea
chimney

techo
roof

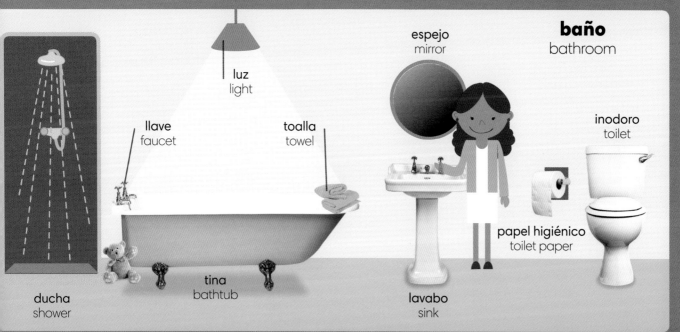

baño
bathroom

espejo
mirror

luz
light

inodoro
toilet

llave
faucet

toalla
towel

papel higiénico
toilet paper

ducha
shower

tina
bathtub

lavabo
sink

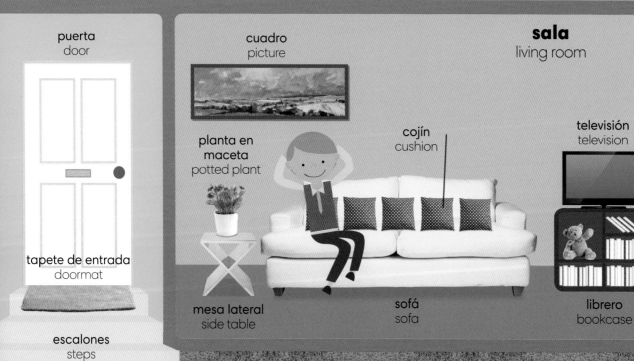

puerta
door

cuadro
picture

sala
living room

televisión
television

planta en
maceta
potted plant

cojín
cushion

tapete de entrada
doormat

mesa lateral
side table

sofá
sofa

librero
bookcase

escalones
steps

19

Juguetes y juegos
Toys and playtime

¿Qué juguete tiene una cola larga y puntiaguda,
y cuál tiene orejas grandes y suaves?
Which toy has a long, spiky tail
and which one has big, soft ears?

tiara
tiara

casco de bombero
firefighter helmet

cometa
kite

disfraz de
princesa
princess
costume

disfraz de bombero
firefighter costume

globos
balloons

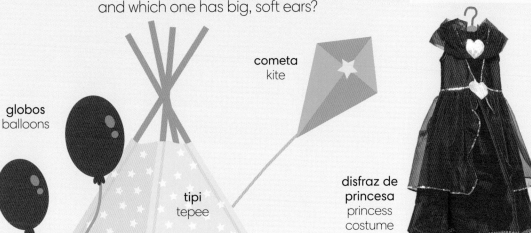

tipi
tepee

pelota
ball

caja para
los juguetes
toy box

muñeca
doll

pandereta
tambourine

tren
train

juego de trenes
train set

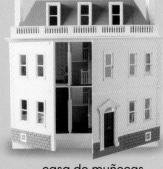

casa de muñecas
dollhouse

vías del tren
train track

caballito mecedor
rocking horse

canicas
marbles

camión de bomberos
fire engine

bloques
blocks

baqueta
drumstick

tambor
drum

juego de té
tea set

rompecabezas
jigsaw puzzle

arcilla para modelar
modeling clay

pato de goma
rubber duck

robot
robot

trompo
top

dinosaurios
dinosaurs

trompeta
trumpet

maza
mallet

xilófono
xylophone

conejo
rabbit

auto
car

oso de peluche
teddy bear

lápices
pencils

bolígrafos
pens

papel
paper

pinceles
paintbrushes

pinturas
paints

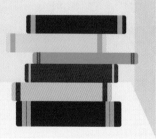
libros
books

Puedo...
I can...

leer un libro
read a book

dibujar
draw pictures

jugar con un juguete
play with a toy

disfrazarme
dress up

tocar música
play music

En la cocina
In the kitchen

pesa
scale

frascos para almacenar
storage jars

rodillo
rolling pin

llave
faucet

pelador
vegetable peeler

tetera
kettle

palillos
chopsticks

lavaplatos líquido
dishwashing liquid

tenedor
fork

plato
plate

pileta
sink

cuchillo
knife

cuchara
spoon

esponjas
sponges

trapo de cocina
dish towel

escurridor
colander

bol para cereal
cereal bowl

trapeador
mop

cubeta
bucket

recogedor y cepillo
dustpan and brush

molde para pastel
cake pan

colador
sieve

taza y plato
cup and saucer

vaso
glass

jarro
jug

batidor
whisk

cuchara de
madera
wooden spoon

hierbas
herbs

cuchillo filoso
sharp knife

tabla para picar
chopping board

tazón
mug

tostador
toaster

sartén
frying pan

bol para mezclar
mixing bowl

rallador
grater

olla
pot

cortadores de galletas
cookie cutters

En la cocina...
In the kitchen we...

preparamos comida
prepare food

cocinamos alimentos
cook meals

horneamos pasteles y golosinas
bake cakes and treats

lavamos los platos
wash dishes

limpiamos
clean

ponemos la mesa
set the table

comemos
eat

tomamos
drink

Busca algo con puntos y algo con rayas.
Find something spotted and something striped.

23

Mascotas favoritas
Favorite pets

¿Qué mascota te gustaría cuidar?
Which pet would you like to care for?

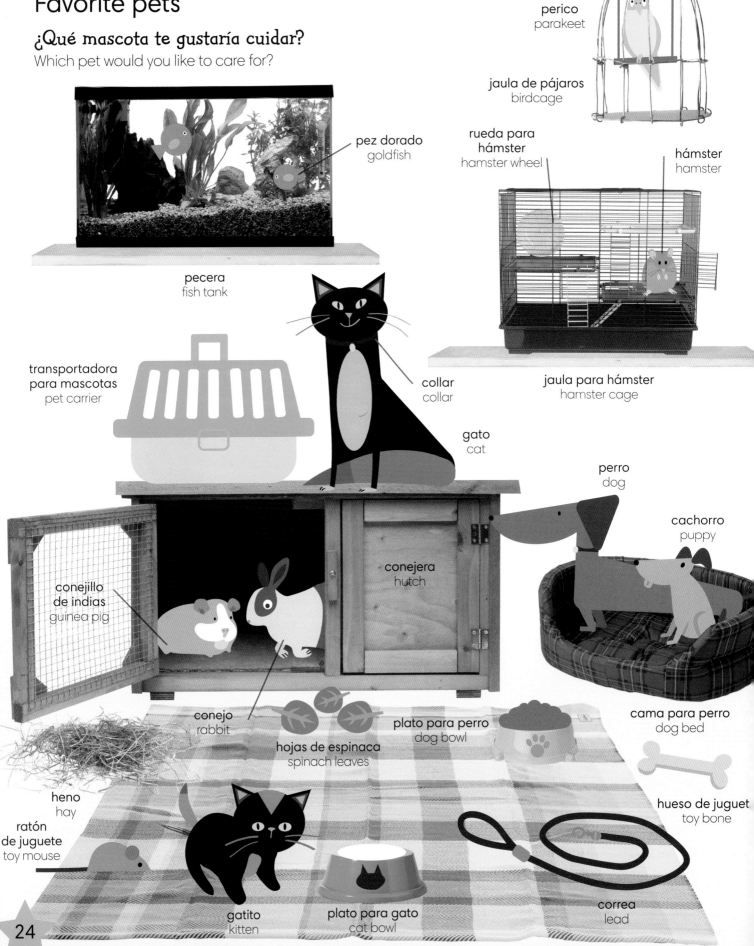

perico
parakeet

jaula de pájaros
birdcage

pez dorado
goldfish

rueda para hámster
hamster wheel

hámster
hamster

pecera
fish tank

transportadora para mascotas
pet carrier

collar
collar

jaula para hámster
hamster cage

gato
cat

perro
dog

cachorro
puppy

conejillo de indias
guinea pig

conejera
hutch

cama para perro
dog bed

conejo
rabbit

hojas de espinaca
spinach leaves

plato para perro
dog bowl

heno
hay

ratón de juguete
toy mouse

hueso de juguet
toy bone

gatito
kitten

plato para gato
cat bowl

correa
lead

El cuento de Tink
Tink's story

Me llamo Tink y soy un perro.
Me encanta perseguir mi pelota
rebotona. ¿A dónde fue?
I'm a dog named Tink. I love
my bouncy ball.
Where did it go?

pelota
rebotona

bouncy
ball

Tink
Tink

**¿Está al lado del gato
dormido?**
Is it by the sleepy cat?

**¿Está arriba de la
conejera?**
Is it on top of the hutch?

gato dormido
sleepy cat

conejera
rabbit hutch

conejo
rabbit

**¿Está en la caja
de arena?**
Is it in the sandbox?

castillos de arena
sandcastles

balde
bucket

caja de arena
sandbox

pala
shovel

banca
bench

**¿Está abajo de la
banca? ¡Sí!**
Is it under the bench?
Yes!

pelota
ball

¡Tink feliz!
happy Tink!

cachorro
amistoso
friendly pup

**¡Guau! ¡Guau!
Mira quién vino a jugar
conmigo a la pelota.**
Woof! Woof! Look who's
come to play ball with me.

25

En el jardín
In the yard

caracol
snail

rama
branch

barda
fence

cobertizo
shed

pajarera
birdhouse

pájaro
bird

arbusto
bush

escoba
broom

tronco del árbol
tree trunk

manguera
hose

césped
lawn

pétalo
petal

carretilla
wheelbarrow

abeja
bee

mariquita
ladybug

regadera
watering can

hoja
leaf

podadora
lawn mower

rosas
roses

pala
trowel

araña
spider

mosca
fly

guantes de jardinería
gardening gloves

telaraña
web

capullo de rosa
rosebud

bulbos
bulbs

26

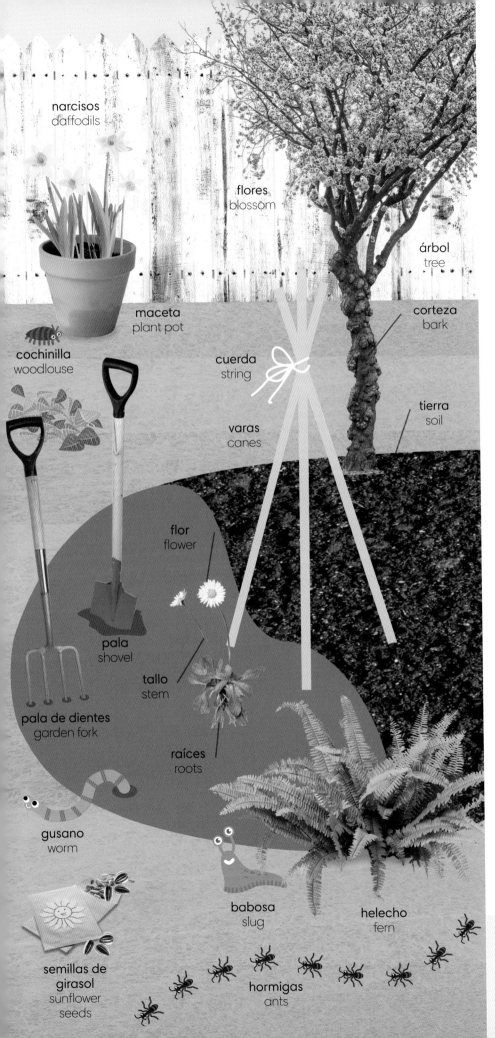

narcisos
daffodils

flores
blossom

árbol
tree

maceta
plant pot

corteza
bark

cochinilla
woodlouse

cuerda
string

tierra
soil

varas
canes

flor
flower

pala
shovel

tallo
stem

pala de dientes
garden fork

raíces
roots

gusano
worm

babosa
slug

helecho
fern

semillas de
girasol
sunflower
seeds

hormigas
ants

excavamos la tierra
dig soil

plantamos semillas y flores
plant seeds and flowers

regamos las plantas
water the plants

podamos el césped
mow the lawn

barremos las hojas
sweep up leaves

¿Qué criatura del jardín tiene ocho patas?
Which garden creature has eight legs?

Describir personas
Describing people

jóvenes
young people

adolescente
adolescent

adultos
grown-ups

adulto
adult

adulta
adult

adulta
adult

niño/niña
child

niño/niña
kid

bebé
baby

niño pequeño
toddler

niño
boy

niña
girl

adolescente
teenager

hombre
man

mujer
woman

anciano/ancian
old person

Los ojos pueden ser...
Eyes can be...

grises
gray

cafés
brown

verdes
green

azules
blue

de color almendrado
hazel

El pelo puede ser...
Hair can be...

¡sin pelo!
gone!

rubio claro
fair

castaño
brown

pelirrojo
red

castaño rojizo
auburn

castaño oscuro
dark brown

calvo
bald

rubio
blond

castaño claro
light brown

gris
gray

corto
short

rizado
curly

liso
straight

cortado en puntas
spiky

largo
long

ondulado
wavy

Elige algunas palabras para describir tu pelo.
Choose some words to describe your hair.

28

Las personas pueden estar/ser...
People can be...

seguras — confident

elegantes — graceful

calmadas — calm

torpes — clumsy

preocupadas — worried

asustadas — scared

serviciales — helpful

golosas — greedy

hambrientas — hungry

amables — kind

bien educadas — polite

felices — happy

tristes — sad

traviesas — naughty

tranquilas — quiet

sorprendidas — surprised

con sueño — asleep

gruñonas — grumpy

despiertas — awake

confundidas — confused

ruidosas — noisy

flojas — lazy

fuertes — strong

chistosas — funny

inteligentes — smart

¿En qué has ayudado hoy?
What helpful things have you done today?

29

En el campo
In the country

pájaros
birds

ciclistas de montaña
mountain bikers

excursionistas
hikers

sendero
trail

puerta
gate

cerca
hedge

tienda de campaña
tent

campistas
camper

zorro
fox

madriguera
burrow

Campamento
Campsite

ramas
sticks

panal
bee's nest

kayak
kayak

flores
flowers

abeja
bee

libélula
dragonfly

brote
bud

huevos
eggs

piña de pino
pine cone

castaña de indias
horse chestnuts

hongo silvestre
wild mushroom

renacuajo
tadpole

¿Qué contiene la semilla de un roble?
What contains the seed of an oak tree?

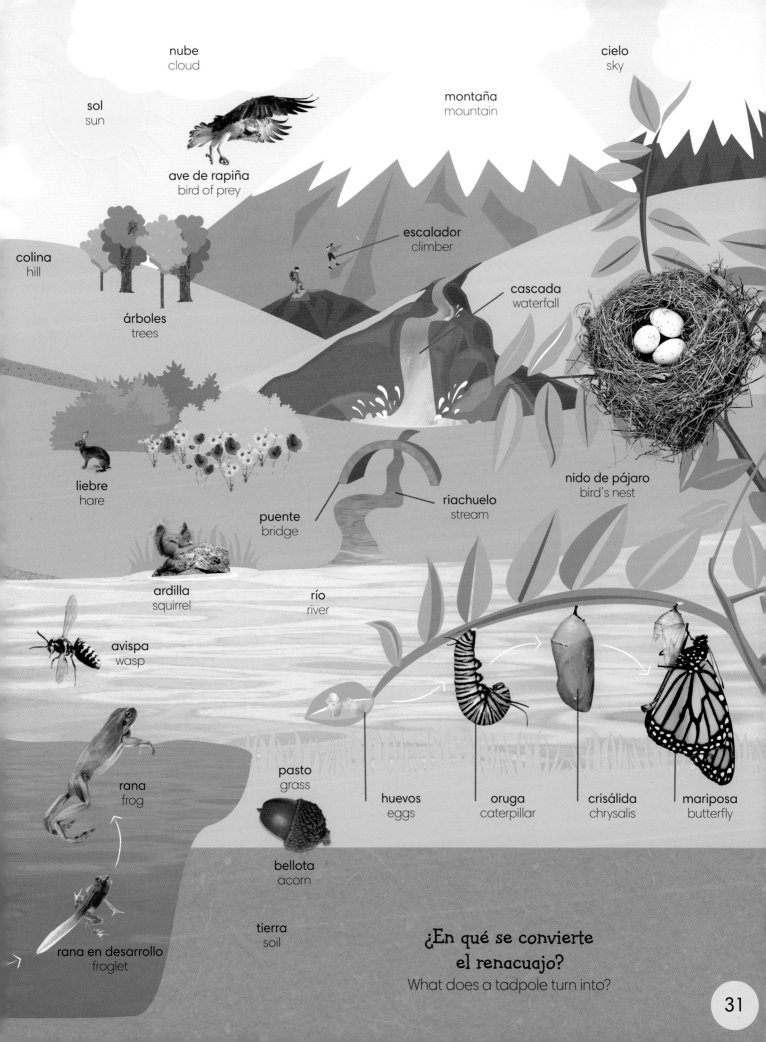

nube
cloud

cielo
sky

sol
sun

montaña
mountain

ave de rapiña
bird of prey

escalador
climber

cascada
waterfall

colina
hill

árboles
trees

nido de pájaro
bird's nest

liebre
hare

riachuelo
stream

puente
bridge

ardilla
squirrel

río
river

avispa
wasp

pasto
grass

huevos
eggs

oruga
caterpillar

crisálida
chrysalis

mariposa
butterfly

rana
frog

bellota
acorn

rana en desarrollo
froglet

tierra
soil

¿En qué se convierte
el renacuajo?
What does a tadpole turn into?

31

En la ciudad
In the city

Elige un lugar que quisieras visitar.
Choose a place you would like to visit.

fuente
fountain

veterinaria
veterinarian's office

teatro
theater

cine
movie theater

restaurante de comida para llevar
takeout restaurant

galería comercial
mall

compradores
shoppers

pastelería
bakery

mercado
market

sinagoga
synagogue

sitio en construcción
construction site

comisaría
police station

consultorio médico
doctor's office

banco
bank

hospital
hospital

museo
museum

carnicería
butcher

dentista
dentist

tienda de abarrotes
grocery store

restaurante
restaurant

calle
road

taxi
taxi

banca
bench

playa
beach

estacionamiento
parking lot

templo
temple

aeropuerto
airport

pista de
aterrizaje
runway

supermercado
supermarket

biblioteca
library

rascacielos
skyscraper

ayuntamiento
town hall

estación de trenes
train station

estatua
statue

castillo saltarín
bouncy castle

resbaladilla
slide

columpio
swing

parque
park

iglesia
church

mezquita
mosque

escuela
school

puente
bridge

cafetería
café

departamentos
apartments

juguetería
toy store

ienda de dulces
candy store

óptica
optician

banqueta
sidewalk

casas
houses

parada
de autobús
bus stop

¿A dónde irías a comer?
Where could you go for some food?

33

Juguemos a la escuelita
Let's play school

La pequeña Ted va a la escuela con su papá.
Little Ted walks to school with her dad.

Papá
Dad

Pequeña Ted
Little Ted

Su maestro le sonríe y la saluda.
Her teacher smiles and says hello.

Hola
Hello

perchas
hooks

Pequeña Ted
Little Ted

mochila
backpack

abrigo
coat

maestro
teacher

La pequeña Ted cuelga su abrigo y su mochila.
Little Ted hangs up her coat and backpack.

hora de cantar
song time

tambor
drum

triángulo
triangle

Todos cantan una canción de buenos días.
Everyone sings a good morning song.

lectura
reading

letras
letters

escribir
writing

abc

Luego, es hora de leer y escribir.
Then it's time for reading and writing.

Después de eso, la pequeña Ted pinta un cuadro.
After that, Little Ted paints a picture.

cuadro
picture

pintar
painting

caballete
easel

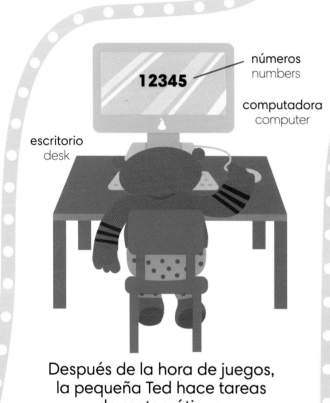

números
numbers

12345

computadora
computer

escritorio
desk

Más tarde, es hora de jugar.
Next it's playtime.

saltar
jumping

rayuela
hopscotch

Después de la hora de juegos, la pequeña Ted hace tareas de matemáticas.
After playtime, Little Ted does number work.

Adiós
Bye-bye

maestro
teacher

amigos
friends

Pequeña Ted
Little Ted

Luego, es hora de irse a casa. La pequeña Ted tiene algunos amigos nuevos.
Then it's time to go home.
Little Ted has made some friends.

En la granja
Around the farm

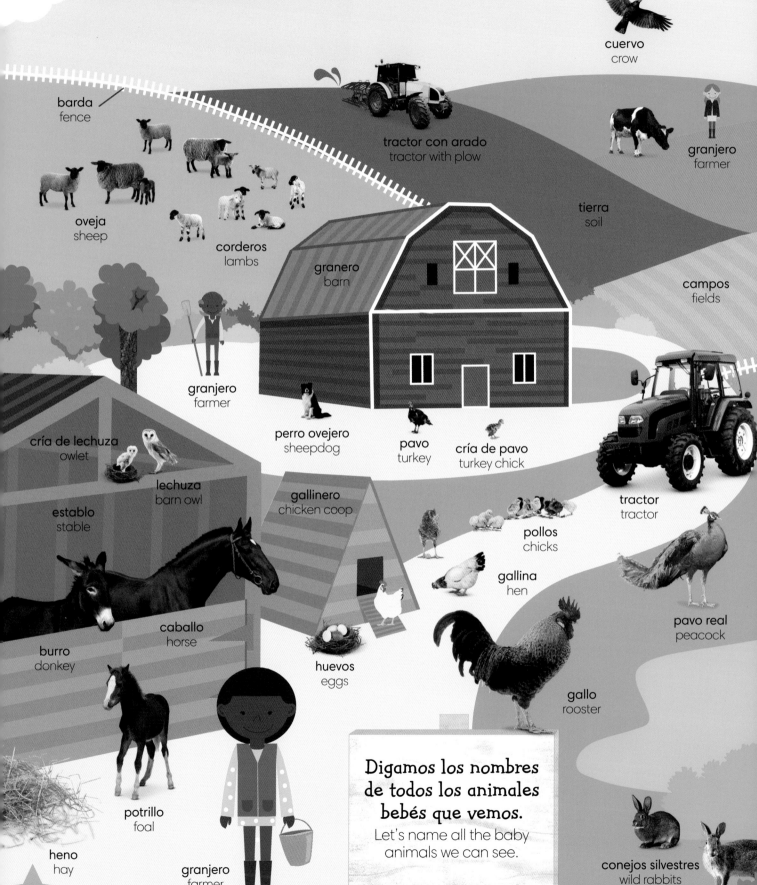

cuervo
crow

barda
fence

tractor con arado
tractor with plow

granjero
farmer

tierra
soil

oveja
sheep

corderos
lambs

granero
barn

campos
fields

granjero
farmer

cría de lechuza
owlet

perro ovejero
sheepdog

pavo
turkey

cría de pavo
turkey chick

tractor
tractor

lechuza
barn owl

gallinero
chicken coop

pollos
chicks

establo
stable

gallina
hen

pavo real
peacock

burro
donkey

caballo
horse

huevos
eggs

gallo
rooster

potrillo
foal

Digamos los nombres
de todos los animales
bebés que vemos.
Let's name all the baby
animals we can see.

conejos silvestres
wild rabbits

heno
hay

granjero
farmer

36

Busca tres granjeros.
Find three farmers.

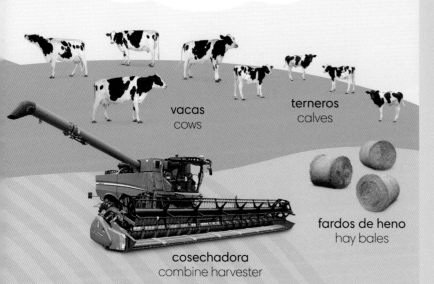

vacas
cows

terneros
calves

cosechadora
combine harvester

fardos de heno
hay bales

porqueriza
pigsty

lodo
mud

cabras
goats

lechones
piglets

cerdos
pigs

cabritos
kids

ganso
goose

patos
ducks

gansito
gosling

patitos
ducklings

abejas
bees

mirlo
blackbird

colmena
beehive

En todo el mundo, los granjeros cultivan...
Around the world, farmers grow...

plantas de arroz
rice plants

aceitunas
olives

maíz
corn

trigo
wheat

manzanas
apples

peras
pears

granos de café
coffee beans

plantas de té
tea plants

piñas
pineapples

plátanos
bananas

Animales salvajes
Animals in the wild

jirafa
giraffe

gaviota
seagull

loro
parrot

venado
deer

chimpancé
chimpanzee

cachorros de león
lion cubs

león
lion

rinoceronte
rhinoceros

elefante
elephant

jaguar
jaguar

camello
camel

kiwi
kiwi

cría de elefante
elephant calf

tortuga de tierra
tortoise

hipopótamo
hippopotamus

panda cachorro
panda cub

cebra
zebra

**Elige tu animal
peludo favorito y...**
Choose your favorite
furry animal and...

potrillo de cebra
zebra foal

ratón
mouse

38

águila
eagle

murciélago
bat

serpiente
snake

koala
koala

mono
monkey

polilla
moth

oso cachorro
bear cub

gorila
gorilla

guepardo
cheetah

lagartija
lizard

araña
spider

oso
bear

canguro
kangaroo

avestruz
ostrich

tigre
tiger

cría de
canguro
joey

flamenco
flamingo

tigre cachorro
tiger cub

rana
frog

lobo
wolf

leopardo
leopard

grillo
cricket

tu animal
con plumas favorito.
your favorite
feathery animal.

escarabajo
beetle

39

Animales de ríos y lagos
River and lake animals

rana
frog

patos reales
mallard ducks

cisnes y
pollos de cisne
swans and
cygnets

caracol
de estanque
pond snail

castor
beaver

nutria
otter

rata de agua
water vole

Busca animales con escamas y...
Find some animals with scales and...

Animales marinos
Sea animals

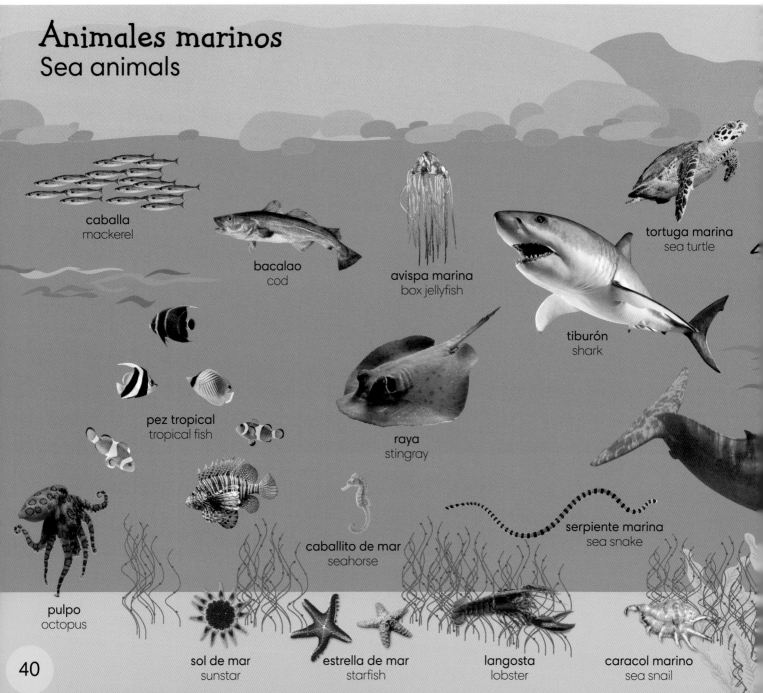

caballa
mackerel

bacalao
cod

avispa marina
box jellyfish

tortuga marina
sea turtle

tiburón
shark

pez tropical
tropical fish

raya
stingray

caballito de mar
seahorse

serpiente marina
sea snake

pulpo
octopus

sol de mar
sunstar

estrella de mar
starfish

langosta
lobster

caracol marino
sea snail

salamandra
newt

caimán
alligator

cocodrilo
crocodile

trucha adulta
adult trout

pececillo
fry

huevos
eggs

carpa
carp

cangrejo de agua dulce
freshwater crab

langosta blanca
crayfish

una palabra para pez bebé.
a word for a baby fish.

pingüino
penguin

lobo marino
sea lion

foca
seal

orca
orca

delfín
dolphin

beluga
beluga whale

ballena azul
blue whale

almeja
clam

navajas
razor clams

camarón
shrimp

jaiba de agua salada
saltwater crab

41

¡A toda velocidad!
Full speed ahead!

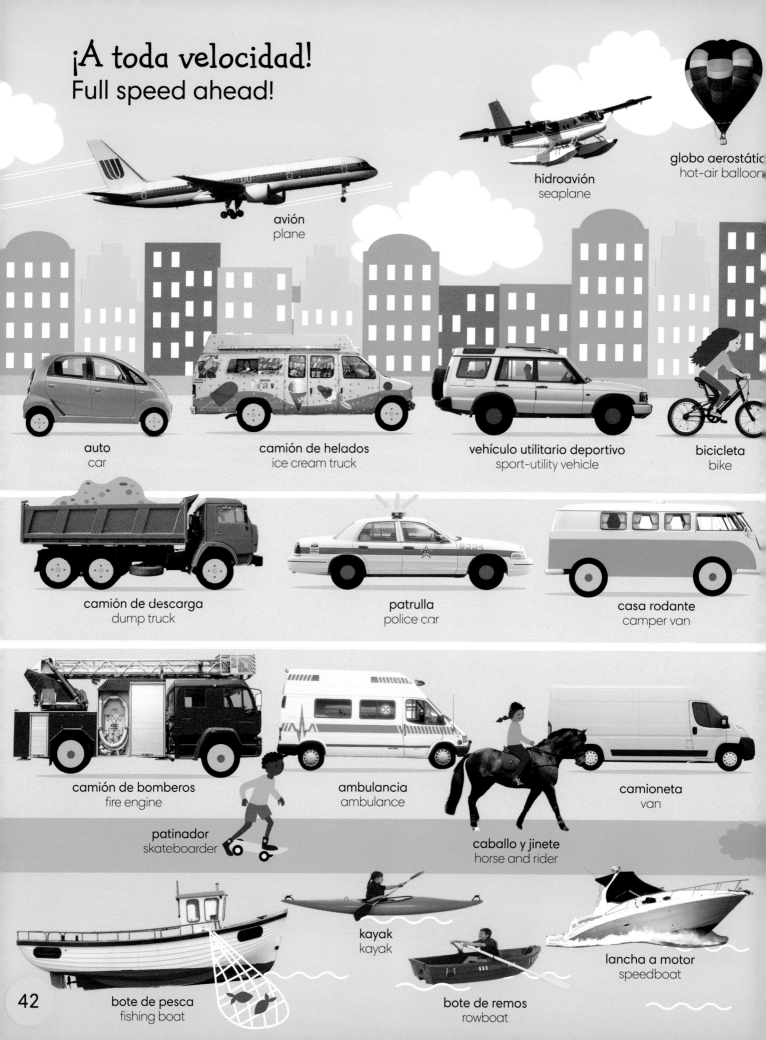

avión
plane

hidroavión
seaplane

globo aerostático
hot-air balloon

auto
car

camión de helados
ice cream truck

vehículo utilitario deportivo
sport-utility vehicle

bicicleta
bike

camión de descarga
dump truck

patrulla
police car

casa rodante
camper van

camión de bomberos
fire engine

ambulancia
ambulance

camioneta
van

patinador
skateboarder

caballo y jinete
horse and rider

kayak
kayak

lancha a motor
speedboat

bote de pesca
fishing boat

bote de remos
rowboat

¿Podríamos manejar, volar o navegar en un bote?
Should we drive, fly, or float in a boat?
Elige un vehículo en el que te gustaría viajar.
Choose a vehicle you would like to travel in.

biplano
biplane

helicóptero de rescate
rescue helicopter

planeador
glider

tren
train

camión de la basura
garbage truck

motocicleta
motorcycle

auto de carrera
race car

tractor
tractor

camión
truck

excavadora
digger

hormigonera
cement mixer

autobús
bus

motoneta
motor scooter

corredor
runner

patinador de monopatín
scooter rider

bote de rescate
rescue boat

velero
sailboat

ferry
ferry

43

¿A dónde iremos?
Where will we go?

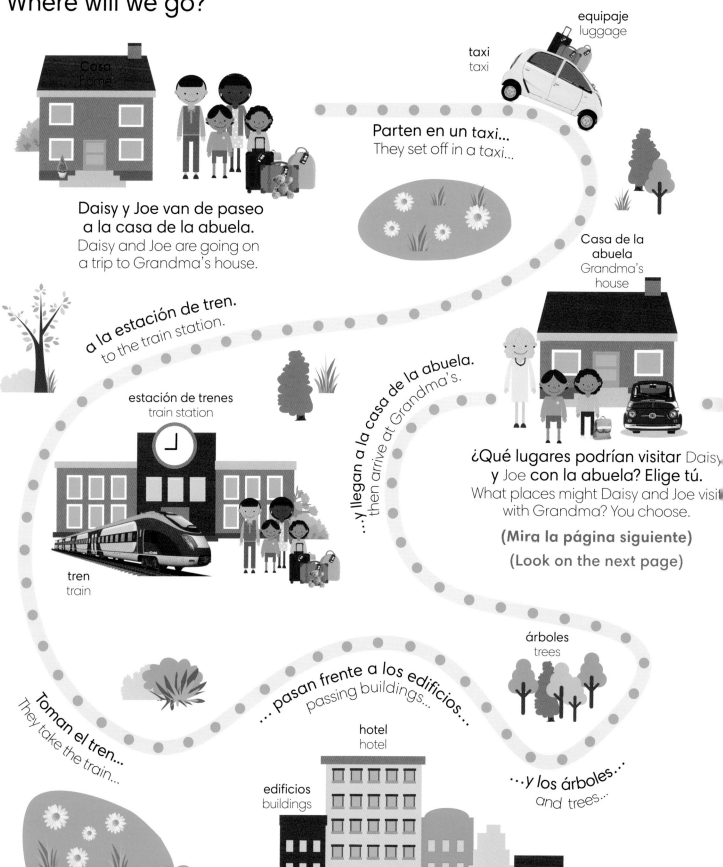

equipaje
luggage

taxi
taxi

Parten en un taxi...
They set off in a taxi...

Casa
home

Daisy y Joe van de paseo
a la casa de la abuela.
Daisy and Joe are going on
a trip to Grandma's house.

Casa de la
abuela
Grandma's
house

a la estación de tren.
to the train station.

estación de trenes
train station

...y llegan a la casa de la abuela.
then arrive at Grandma's.

¿Qué lugares podrían visitar Daisy
y Joe con la abuela? Elige tú.
What places might Daisy and Joe visit
with Grandma? You choose.

(Mira la página siguiente)

(Look on the next page)

tren
train

árboles
trees

... pasan frente a los edificios...
passing buildings...

Toman el tren...
They take the train...

hotel
hotel

edificios
buildings

...y los árboles...
and trees...

44

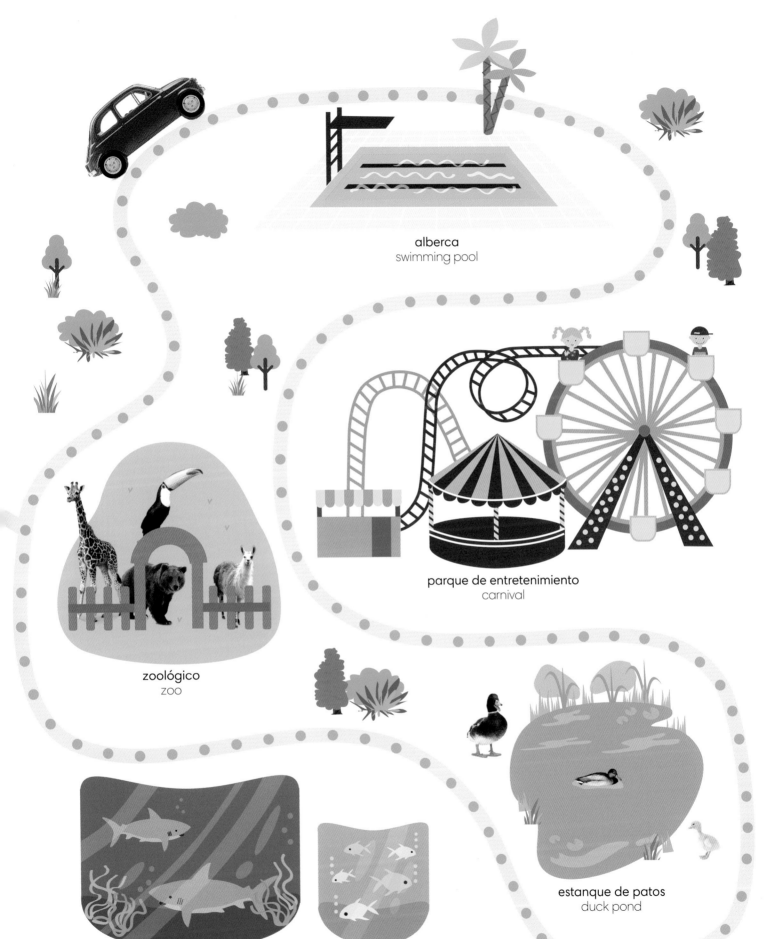

alberca
swimming pool

parque de entretenimiento
carnival

zoológico
zoo

acuario
aquarium

estanque de patos
duck pond

¡Palabras ruidosas!
Noisy words!

¡plic! ¡ploc!
pitter! patter!

¡tuturutú!
toot! toot!

¡ring! ¡ring!
ring! ring!

¡chif!
¡chof!
splish!
splash!

¡PLAF!
WHAM!
¡CLONC!
KAPOW!

¡tic-tac!
tick-tock!

¡bruuuum!
neeaoooowww!

¡uuuh! ¡uuuh!
woooh! woooh!

¡tilín!
¡tilín!
jingle!
jingle!

¡pu pu! ¡pu pu!
choo! choo!

¿Qué hace un sonido ruidoso?
What makes a noisy sound?

¡cua!
¡cua!
quack!
quack!

¡cloc!
¡cloc!
cluck! cluck!

¡GRRRR!
ROAR!

¡pío!
¡pío!
cheep!
cheep!

¡cruac!
squawk!

46

¡blip!
¡ping!
bleep! iping!

¡pop!
¡bang!
pop! bang!

¡toc!
¡toc!
tap! tap!

¡braaa! ¡braaa!
trompety
trump!

¡bruuum!
¡bip! ¡bip!
brmm! beep! beep!

¿Qué hace un sonido suave?
What makes a quiet sound?

¡muuu!
moo!

¡auuu!
hoooowl!

¡oinc! ¡oinc!
oink! oink!

¡Guau! ¡Guau!
woof! woof!

¡iiiiih!
neigh!

¡beee!
baa!

¡glu! gobble!

¡croac! ¡croac!
ribbit!
ribbit!

¡pío!
tweet!

¡pío!
tweet!

¡uh uh!
hoot-hoot!

¡uh uh!¡ uh uh!
ooh! ooh! ooh!

¡zzzzzz!
buzzzzz!

¡sssssss!
hissssss!

¡Palabras ruidosas de los animales!
Noisy animal words!

¡miau!
meow!

¡clic!
¡clic!
squeak!
squeak!

¡quiquiriquí!
cock-a-doodle-doo!

47

En qué trabajan las personas
What people do

¿A qué te gustaría dedicarte?
What job would you like to do?

bombero
firefighter

doctora
doctor

enfermero
nurse

diseñadora de moda
fashion designer

cantante
singer

científica
scientist

música
musician

dentista
dentist

DJ (disc jockey)
DJ (disc jockey)

artista
artist

peluquero
hairdresser

actriz
actor

astronauta
astronaut

constructor
builder

maestro
teacher

bibliotecario
librarian

piloto
pilot

veterinario
vet

directora de cine
film director

futbolista
soccer player

chef
chef

soldado
soldier

abogada
lawyer

deportista
athlete

bailarín
dancer

policía
police officer

niñera
babysitter

tenista
tennis player

ingeniera
engineer

presidenta
president

escritora
writer

Algunos pasatiempos
Some hobbies

gimnasia
gymnastics

artes marciales
martial arts

música
music

baile
dancing

natación
swimming

Todo tipo de lugares
All sorts of places

Luna
moon

cometa
comet

Lugar frío
Cold place

iglú
igloo

pesca en el hielo
ice fishing

oso polar
polar bear

Imagina que estás en una aventura.
Imagine you are on an adventure.

¿A dónde irías?
Where will you go?

Sabana
Savanna

leones
lions

antílope
antelope

pastizales
grasses

Océano
Ocean

buzo
diver

coral
coral

pez
fish

barco naufragado
shipwreck

tiburón
shark

lecho marino
seabed

50

Tierra
Earth

transbordador
espacial
space shuttle

estrellas
stars

Espacio
Space

cohete
rocket

Sol
sun

Desierto
Desert

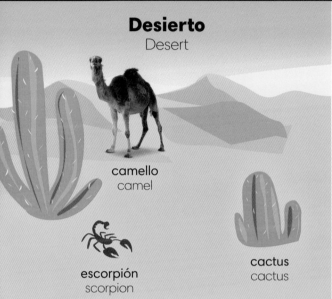

camello
camel

escorpión
scorpion

cactus
cactus

loro
parrot

árbol
tree

tarántula
tarantula

telaraña
web

Selva
Rain forest

Algunas características
de la tierra y la costa
Some land and shore features

montañas
mountains

valles
valley

lago
lake

isla
island

volcán
volcano

playa
beach

acantilado
cliff

desembocadura
estuary

51

Colores, formas y números
Colors, shapes, and numbers

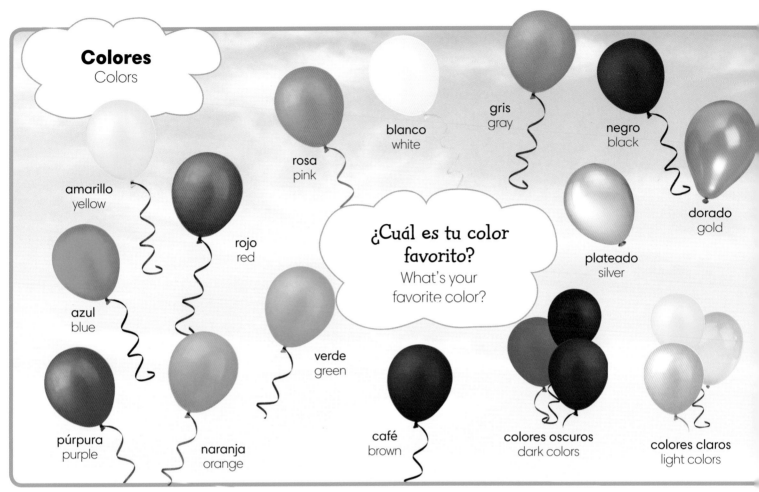

Colores
Colors

amarillo
yellow

rojo
red

azul
blue

púrpura
purple

naranja
orange

rosa
pink

blanco
white

verde
green

café
brown

gris
gray

negro
black

plateado
silver

dorado
gold

colores oscuros
dark colors

colores claros
light colors

¿Cuál es tu color favorito?
What's your favorite color?

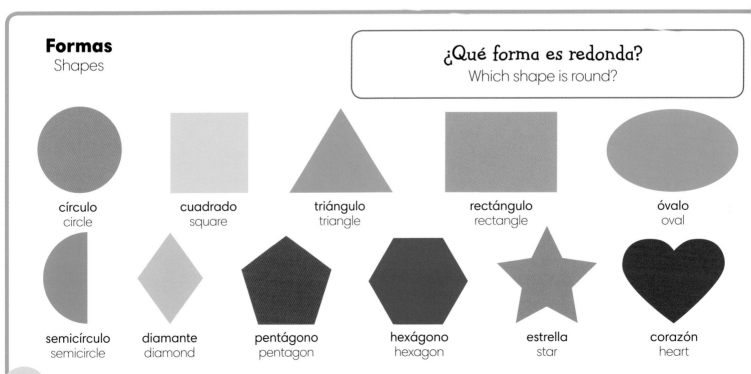

Formas
Shapes

¿Qué forma es redonda?
Which shape is round?

círculo
circle

cuadrado
square

triángulo
triangle

rectángulo
rectangle

óvalo
oval

semicírculo
semicircle

diamante
diamond

pentágono
pentagon

hexágono
hexagon

estrella
star

corazón
heart

Números
Numbers

0
cero
zero

1
uno
one

2
dos
two

3
tres
three

4
cuatro
cuatro

5
cinco
five

6
seis
six

7
siete
seven

8
ocho
eight

9
nueve
nine

10
diez
ten

11
once
eleven

12
doce
twelve

13
trece
thirteen

14
catorce
fourteen

15
quince
fifteen

16
dieciséis
sixteen

17
diecisiete
seventeen

18
dieciocho
eighteen

19
diecinueve
nineteen

20
veinte
twenty

100
cien
one hundred

1000
mil
one thousand

1000000
un millón
one million

Época, estaciones y tiempo
Time, seasons, and weather

día
daytime

noche
nighttime

Días
Days

Lunes
Monday

Martes
Tuesday

Miércoles
Wednesday

Jueves
Thursday

Viernes
Friday

Sábado
Saturday

Domingo
Sunday

Meses
Months

Enero
January

Febrero
February

Marzo
March

Abril
April

Mayo
May

Junio
June

Julio
July

Agosto
August

Septiembre
September

Octubre
October

Noviembre
November

Diciembre
December

Estaciones
Seasons

Primavera
Spring

Verano
Summer

Otoño
Fall

Invierno
Winter

¿En qué mes es tu cumpleaños?
What month is your birthday?

Algunas celebraciones
Some celebrations

Cumpleaños
Birthdays

Eid
Eid

Diwali
Diwali

Navidad
Christmas

Hanukkah
Hanukkah

Año Nuevo chino
Chinese New Year

Tiempo
Weather

caluroso
hot

soleado
sunny

frío
cold

con nieve
snowy

húmedo
wet

plic
ploc
pitter
patter
lluvioso
rainy

seco
dry

despejado
blue skies

arcoíris
rainbow

¡paf!
splish!
¡zas!
splash!
charcos
puddles

¡bang! ¡pum!
rumble!
boom!
rayos y truenos
thunder and lightning

tormentoso
stormy

nublado
cloudy

con brisa
breezy

¡fiuuuu!
whoosh!
con viento
windy

granizo
hail

con neblina
foggy

con escarcha
frosty

helado
icy

tormenta de nieve
blizzard

¿Cómo está el tiempo hoy?
What's the weather like today?

La hora de los cuentos
Story time

hada
fairy

gato de la bruja
witch's cat

bruja
witch

hada madrina
fairy godmother

unicornio
unicorn

extraterrestre
alien

escoba
broomstick

corona
crown

caldero
cauldron

princesa
princess

príncipe
prince

reina
queen

rey
king

palacio
palace

criado
servant

sapo
toad

ratón
mouse

zapato de cristal
glass slipper

caballo y carruaje
horse and carriage

varita mágica
wand

lobo
wolf

superhéroe
superhero

explorador
explorer

bestia
beast

mago
wizard

el malo
bad guy

cueva
cave

¿Quién viaja en escoba? ¿Quién usa la corona?
Who rides a broomstick? Who wears a crown?

gigante
giant

genio
genie

lámpara
lamp

monstruo
monster

alfombra
mágica
magic carpet

castillo
castle

armadura
armor

fantasma
ghost

espada
sword

caballero
knight

escudo
shield

dragón
dragon

torre
tower

espía
spy

dinosaurio
dinosaur

pirata
pirate

loro
parrot

barco pirata
pirate ship

tesoro
treasure

frijoles mágicos
beanstalk

sirena
mermaid

monedas
coins

cofre del tesoro
treasure chest

57

Inventemos un cuento
Let's make up a story

El principio
The beginning

Había una vez...
Once upon a time...

(ahora elige un personaje)
(now choose a character)

o
or

**un valiente
caballero...**
a brave knight...

**una
superheroína...**
a superhero...

¿Qué les pasa?
What happens to them?

Decide tú.
You choose.

hielo
ice

está congelado/a en hielo.
is frozen in ice.

**se queda dormido/a
y no puede despertar.**
falls asleep and
can't wake up.

micrófono
microphone

**no puede dejar de
cantar.**
can't stop singing.

manzana
apple

grande
big

pequeño
small

diminuto
tiny

come una manzana y se encoge.
eats an apple and shrinks.

¿Con quién se encuentran?
Who do they meet?
Decide tú. Aparece...
You choose. Along comes...

un robot útil.
a helpful robot.

máquina reiniciadora
rebooting machine

una bruja
amable.
a kind witch.

¿Qué pasa después?
What happens next?

La máquina reiniciadora del robot
arregla todo.
The robot's rebooting machine
puts everything right.

varita mágica
wand

**libro
de hechizos**
spell book

¿Cómo termina?
How does it end?

Un hechizo mágico arregla todo.
A magic spell puts everything right.

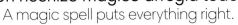

amigos felices
happy friends

palacio mágico
magical palace

Viven felices y comen perdices
en un palacio mágico con sus amigos.
They live happily ever after in a magical
palace with all their friends.

59

¡Palabras maravillosas!
Wonderful words!
¿Te has preguntado **alguna vez**... / Have you ever **wondered**...

qué son las palabras?
what words are?

Escuchamos cómo **suenan** las palabras.
We hear words as **sounds**.

¡Hola!
hello!

Las escribimos usando **símbolos**.
We write them using **symbols**.

perro
dog

En español, los símbolos se llaman **letras**.
In English the symbols are called **letters**.

para qué sirven las palabras?
what words are for?

Todas las palabras **significan** algo.

All words **mean** something.

manzana
apple

Manzana significa una fruta jugosa y crujiente que es redonda y crece en un árbol.
Apple means a crunchy, juicy fruit that's round and grows on a tree.

qué hacen las palabras?
what words do?

Las palabras tienen **distintas funciones** en una oración.
Words do **different jobs** in a sentence.

Las palabras que **nombran** las cosas se llaman **sustantivos**.
Words that **name** things are called **nouns**.

¿Puedes buscar estos **sustantivos** en este libro?

Can you find these **nouns** in this book?

niña
girl

tractor
tractor

polilla
moth

sapo
toad

helado
ice cream

Las palabras que te dicen lo que está **haciendo** algo se llaman **verbos**.
Words that tell you what something is **doing** are called **verbs**.

¿Puedes buscar estos **verbos** en este libro?

Can you find these **verbs** in this book?

caminar
walk

dibujar
draw

ver
seeing

saltar
jumping

saborear
tasting

Las palabras que **describen** cómo es algo se llaman **adjetivos**.
Words that **describe** what something is like are called **adjectives**.

¿Puedes buscar estos **adjetivos** en este libro?

Can you find these **adjectives** in this book?

húmedo
wet

rizado
curly

fuertes
strong

felices
happy

rebotona
bouncy

Agradecimientos / Acknowledgments

The publisher would like to thank the following for their kind permission to reproduce their photographs:

(Key: a=above; b=below/bottom; c=center; f=far; l=left; r=right; t=top)

5 Dreamstime.com: Mikelane45 (clb). **6 123RF.com:** Rawan Hussein | designsstock (fclb/ice cream, fcr); Sataporn Jiwjalaen (ca); Ruslan Iefremov / Ruslaniefremov (fcra). **Dorling Kindersley:** Natural History Museum, London (fcl/butterfly); Tata Motors (fcla, fbl/Nano); Gary Ombler / Lister Wilder (clb). **Dreamstime.com:** Jessamine (fbl, crb). **7 Dorling Kindersley:** Natural History Museum, London (fclb); Tata Motors (bc). **8 123RF.com:** 6440925 (fbl); Belchonock (bc/Sun screen); Pixelrobot (fbr); Kornienko (bc). **Dreamstime.com:** Georgii Dolgykh / Gdolgikh (br). **10 123RF.com:** Piotr Pawinski / ppart (fcla/Green, fcl/Red, fclb/Brown, fclb/Purple). **10–11 Dreamstime.com:** Fibobjects (b/Flowers). **11 123RF.com:** Piotr Pawinski / ppart (tr/Grey, cr/Blue); Anatolii Tsekhmister / tsekhmister (tr). **Dreamstime.com:** Piyagoon (crb). **Fotolia:** Fotojagodka (tr/Cat). **12 123RF.com:** Murali Nath / muralinathypr (clb); Punkbarby (fcl). **Dreamstime.com:** Milos Tasic / Tale (clb/Sport Shoes). **13 123RF.com:** Burnel1 (tc); Natthawut Panyosaeng / aopsan (ca); Sataporn Jiwjalaen (bc). **Dreamstime.com:** Chiyacat (cra). **iStockphoto.com:** Tarzhanova (fcra). **14 123RF.com:** Angelstorm (cra/Strawberries); Rose-Marie Henriksson / rosemhenri (fcrb/Cupcakes); Belchonock (bc/Celery). **Dreamstime.com:** Tracy Decourcy / Rimglow (fcr/Carrot); Leszek Ogrodnik / Lehu (cra/Apple, fcra/Orange, c/Red Pepper, cb/Broccoli, crb/Cabbage); Elena Schweitzer / Egal (cra/Cauliflower, bc/Lettuce); Grafner (br). **15 123RF.com:** Karammiri (clb); Utima (bl). **Alamy Stock Photo:** Peter Vrabel (br). **Dreamstime.com:** Denlarkin (fclb); Tarapatta (ca); Pogonici (cla/Yogurt). **17 123RF.com:** Evgeny Karandaev (tl). **18 123RF.com:** Andriy Popov (cb). **18–19 Dreamstime.com:** Hai Huy Ton That / Huytonthat (b). **19 Dreamstime.com:** Jamie Cross (crb); Svetlana Voronina (ca); Kettaphoto (clb). **20 Dreamstime.com:** Stephanie Frey (cr); Thomas Perkins / Perkmeup (crb). **21 123RF.com:** Birgit Korber / 2005kbphotodesign (c). **Dorling Kindersley:** Toymaker, Jomanda (fcr). **Dreamstime.com:** Thomas Perkins / Perkmeup (fbr). **24 Dreamstime.com:** Photka (br). **26–27 123RF.com:** Leo Lintang (t). **Dreamstime.com:** Hai Huy Ton That / Huytonthat. **26 123RF.com:** Dmitriy Syechin / alexan66 (clb, bl); Singkam Chanteb (cra). **Dreamstime.com:** Aprescindere (bc, bc/Rose); Fibobjects (cra); Aleksandr Jocic (c); Danny Smythe / Rimglow (crb). **AA Photolibrary:** Stockbyte (bl). **27 123RF.com:** Lev Kropotov (tc); Keatanan Viya (cb). **Dreamstime.com:** Andreykuzmin (c); Andrzej Tokarski (cl). **30 123RF.com:** Sergey Kolesnikov (cb); Oksana Tkachuk / ksena32 (clb). **Dreamstime.com:** Steve Allen / Mrallen (cra/Kelp Gull); Liligraphie (cra); Sergey Uryadnikov / Surz01 (tr); N Van D / Nataliavand (clb/Poppy); Isselee (br). **30–31 Fotolia:** Malbert. **iStockphoto.com:** T_Kimura (t). **31 123RF.com:** Oksana Tkachuk / ksena32 (cla, cb). **Dreamstime.com:** Stephanie Frey (cra); N Van D / Nataliavand (cl, c, clb); Stevenrussellsmithphotos (crb). **iStockphoto.com:** Aluxum (clb/Frog). **36 123RF.com:** BenFoto (crb/Peacock); Ron Rowan / framed1 (br, br/Rabbit). **Dorling Kindersley:** Philip Dowell (cla, cla/Sheep). **Dreamstime.com:** Anagram1 (tr); Eric Isselee (clb); Jessamine (cb); Oleksandr Lytvynenko / Voren1 (cb/Chicken); Goce Risteski (ca); Photobac (crb). **37 123RF.com:** Eric Isselee / isselee (cla); Eric Isselee / isselee (cla/Veal); Alexey Zarodov / Rihardzz (cra/haystack). **Dorling Kindersley:** Alan Buckingham (cr); Doubleday Swineshead Depot (ca/Combine Harvester). **Dreamstime.com:** Eric Isselee (cla/cow); Eric Isselee (c); Yphotoland (crb); Just_Regress (cra); Damian Palus (ca). **Fotolia:** Eric Isselee (ca/cow). **Getty Images:** Dougal Waters / Photographer's Choice RF (br). **38 123RF.com:** Duncan Noakes (cl); Andrejs Pidjass / NejroN (tc); Ana Vasileva / ABV (c). **Dorling Kindersley:** Andrew Beckett (Illustration Ltd) (cr); British Wildlife Centre, Surrey, UK (cra/Deer). **Dreamstime.com:** Justin Black / Jblackstock (br); Eric Isselee / Isselee (fcl); Cynoclub (bl); Isselee (fcla). **Fotolia:** Eric Isselee (cra/Lion Cubs); Valeriy Kalyuzhnyy / StarJumper (tl); shama65 (cla); Eric Isselee (fbl); Eric Isselee (bc); Jan Will (fbr). **39 123RF.com:** Vitalii Gulay / vitalisg (cla/Lizard); smileus (cr); / Ermolaev Alexandr Alexandrovich / photodeti (tc); Alexey Sholom (cl). **Dorling Kindersley:** Natural History Museum, London (cra/moth). **Dreamstime.com:** Hel080808 (crb); Brandon Smith / Bgsmith (ca); Goinyk Volodymyr (tr); Ryan Pike / Cre8tive_studios (cla); Kazoka (cb); Valeriy Kalyuzhnyy / Dragoneye (clb). **Fotolia:** Eric Isselee (tr/Koala); Eric Isselee (bc). **Photolibrary:** Digital Vision / Martin Harvey (clb/Tige Cub). **40 Alamy Stock Photo:** Rosanne Tackaberry (fcla). **Dorling Kindersley:** Weymouth Sea Life Centre (fclb). **Dreamstime.com:** Andybignellphoto (fcra); Paul Farnfield (ca); Jnjhuz (cra); Isselee (cr); Elvira Kolomiytseva (cb); Cynoclub (clb/Lionfish); Veruska1969 (bc); Ethan Daniels (crb); Berczy04 (br); Richard Carey (cr). **iStockphoto.com:** Alxpin (clb). **41 Alamy Stock Photo:** WaterFrame (cb/Blue Whale). **Dreamstime.com:** Tom Ashton (tc); Matthijs Kuijpers (tc); Chinnasorn Pangcharoen (tr); Margo555 (cla); Lext (ca); Vladimir Blinov (fcla); Snyfer (ca/Sea lion); Isselee (cra/Seal); Musat Christian (fcl); Caan2gobelow (cr). **iStockphoto.com:** Cmeder (cb). **42 123RF.com:** Gary Blakeley (br/Speedboat); Veniamin Kraskov (cl); Somjring Chuankul (clb); Kzenon (crb). **Dorling Kindersley:** Tata Motors (cla). **Dreamstime.com:** Maria Feklistova (tc); Melonstone (bl). **43 123RF.com:** Artem Konovalov (cr); Nerthuz (cla). **Corbis:** Terraqua Images (ca). **Dorling Kindersley:** Hitachi Rail Europe (fcra). **Dreamstime.com:** Eugenesergeev (br); Shariff Che\' Lah (cra); Mlan61 (cb). **New Holland Agriculture:** (fcl). **44 123RF.com:** Scanrail (clb/Train). **Dorling Kindersley:** Andy Crawford / Janet and Roger Westcott (cr/Car); Tata Motors (tr). **Dreamstime.com:** Fibobjects (bl, cra). **45 123RF.com:** Acceptphoto (clb/Llama). **Alamy Stock Photo:** Rosanne Tackaberry (crb/Duck). **Dorling Kindersley:** Andy Crawford / Janet and Roger Westcott (tl). **46 123RF.com:** Lev Dolgachov (fclb); Olaf Schulz / Schulzhattingen (c). **Dreamstime.com:** Fotomirc (bc/Rooster); Jmsakura / John Mills (cr); Eric Isselee (bc); Isselee (br). **Fotolia:** Malbert (cb/Water). **Getty Images:** Don Farrall / Photodisc (cb). **46–47 Dreamstime.com:** Glinn (b). **47 Dorling Kindersley:** Odds Farm Park, Buckinghamshire (ca/Pig). **Dreamstime.com:** Anna Utekhina / Anna63 (bl); Maksim Toome / Mtoome (cla); Yudesign (tc); Uros Petrovic / Urospetrovic (fcra); Eric Isselee (fcra/Cow); Chris Lorenz / Chrislorenz (ca); Rudmer Zwerver / Creativenature1 (fcrb); Mikelane45 (bc). **50 Dorling Kindersley:** Greg and Yvonne Dean (crb); Jerry Young (ca). **51 Dreamstime.com:** Ali Ender Birer / Enderbirer (tl). **52 Dreamstime.com:** Alinamd (t); Snake3d (cra). **53 123RF.com:** Dmitriy Syechin / alexan66 (cr); Jessmine (fcra). **Dreamstime.com:** Dibrova (fcr); Jlcst (cl); Ralf Neumann / Ingwio (cra); Irochka (c); Qpicimages (cr/Hibiscus leaf); Paulpaladin (cr/Mint Leaf). **54 123RF.com:** Mikekiev (r). **55 Dorling Kindersley:** Andy Crawford / Janet and Roger Westcott (bl). **56 123RF.com:** Eric Isselee (cla); Boris Medvedev (c). **Dreamstime.com:** Iakov Filimonov (cb); Alexander Potapov (cl/Shoe). **Fotolia:** Malbert (cl). **Getty Images:** C Squared Studios / Photodisc (ca). **56–57 iStockphoto.com:** Rodnikovay. **57 123RF.com:** Andreykuzmin (ca/Shield); Blueringmedia (tr); Oliver Lenz (l); Konstantin Shaklein (cb); Jehsomwang (crb). **Depositphotos Inc:** mreco99 (cra). **Dorling Kindersley:** Wallace Collection, London (ca/Armour). **Fotolia:** Malbert (ca). **60 Dorling Kindersley:** Natural History Museum, London (cb). **Dreamstime.com:** Artigiano (crb/Strawberry); Grafner (crb). **New Holland Agriculture:** (cb/Tractor). **61 123RF.com:** Scanrail (fcra). **Dorling Kindersley:** Natural History Museum, London (fclb); Tata Motors (bc, fcrb). **Dreamstime.com:** Jessamine (bl, fcrb/Nest)

Cover images: *Front:* **123RF.com:** Parinya Binsuk / parinyabinsuk cb, Ruslan Iefremov / Ruslaniefremov clb/ (fountain), Scanrail cb/ (train); **Corbis:** Terraqua Images clb/ (helicopter); **Dorling Kindersley:** Natural History Museum, London tl/ (butterfly), Tata Motors tr; **Dreamstime.com:** Andygaylor clb, Borislav Borisov cb/ (bird), Jessamine tl, Anke Van Wyk tl; **iStockphoto.com:** ZargonDesign cl; *Back:* **123RF.com:** Parinya Binsuk / parinyabinsuk cb, Rawan Hussein | designsstock cl/ (ice cream), Ruslan Iefremov / Ruslaniefremov clb/ (fountain), Sataporn Jiwjalaen / onairjiw tl/ (sunglasses), Scanrail cb/ (train); **Corbis:** Terraqua Images clb/ (helicopter); **Dorling Kindersley:** Natural History Museum, London cra, Tata Motors tr; **Dreamstime.com:** Andygaylor clb, Borislav Borisov cb/ (bird), Xaoc tl; **iStockphoto.com:** ZargonDesign cl

All other images © Dorling Kindersley

¡Sigue aprendiendo palabras! Son muy **útiles.**

Keep learning words! They are very **useful.**

61